FOLLOW THAT TAP WATER!

A JOURNEY DOWN THE DRAIN

KEEPING CITIES CLEAN

BY BRIDGET HEOS • ILLUSTRATED BY ALEX WESTGATE

AMICUS ILLUSTRATED AND AMICUS INK
are published by Amicus
P.O. Box 227, Mankato, MN 56002
www.amicuspublishing.us

Paperback edition: ISBN 978-1-62243-354-4

LIBRARY OF CONGRESS CATALOGING-IN-PUBLICATION DATA
Names: Heos, Bridget, author.
Title: Follow that tap water! : a journey down the drain / by Bridget Heos.
Description: Mankato, Minnesota : Amicus, [2017] | Series: Keeping cities clean | Series: Amicus illustrated | Audience: K to grade 3. | Includes bibliographical references and index.
Identifiers: LCCN 2015040632 (print) | LCCN 2015041789 (ebook) | ISBN 9781607539629 (library binding : alk. paper) | ISBN 9781681510804 (eBook)
Subjects: LCSH: Water-supply—Juvenile literature. | Water reuse—Juvenile literature. | Water conservation—Juvenile literature. | Sewage—Juvenile literature.
Classification: LCC TD348 .H46 2017 (print) | LCC TD348 (ebook) | DDC 363.6/1—dc23
LC record available at http://lccn.loc.gov/2015040632

EDITOR: Rebecca Glaser
DESIGNER: Kathleen Petelinsek

ABOUT THE AUTHOR

Bridget Heos lives in Kansas City with her husband and four children. She has written more than 80 books for children, including several about the Earth and the environment. Find out more about her at www.authorbridgetheos.com.

ABOUT THE ILLUSTRATOR

Alex Westgate is an illustrator, designer, and artist from Toronto, Ontario, Canada. He has worked for *The Washington Post*, BBC, *Reader's Digest*, and more. He drinks tap water, recycles, and throws things in the garbage every day.

Swish! When you help wash the dishes, the dirty dishwater goes down the drain. Have you ever wondered where it goes after that? Let's follow a few drops of water and see!

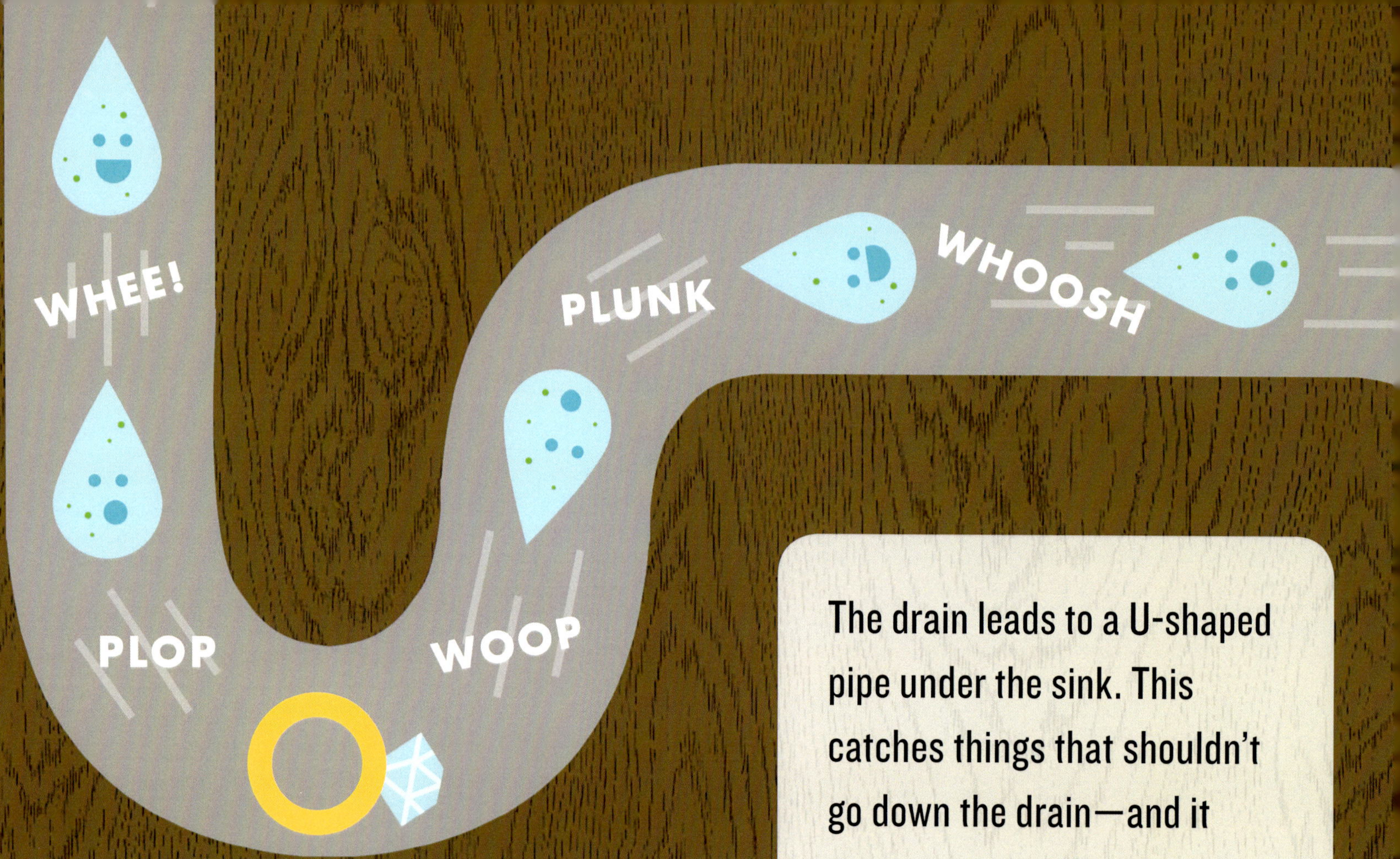

The drain leads to a U-shaped pipe under the sink. This catches things that shouldn't go down the drain—and it stops sewer smells from coming back into your house!

Then the water goes straight down the drainpipe. It's like a superfast slide! The water reaches a new pipe under the house and changes direction. This pipe takes water out of the house. The pipe slopes slightly downward so that the water flows gently downhill.

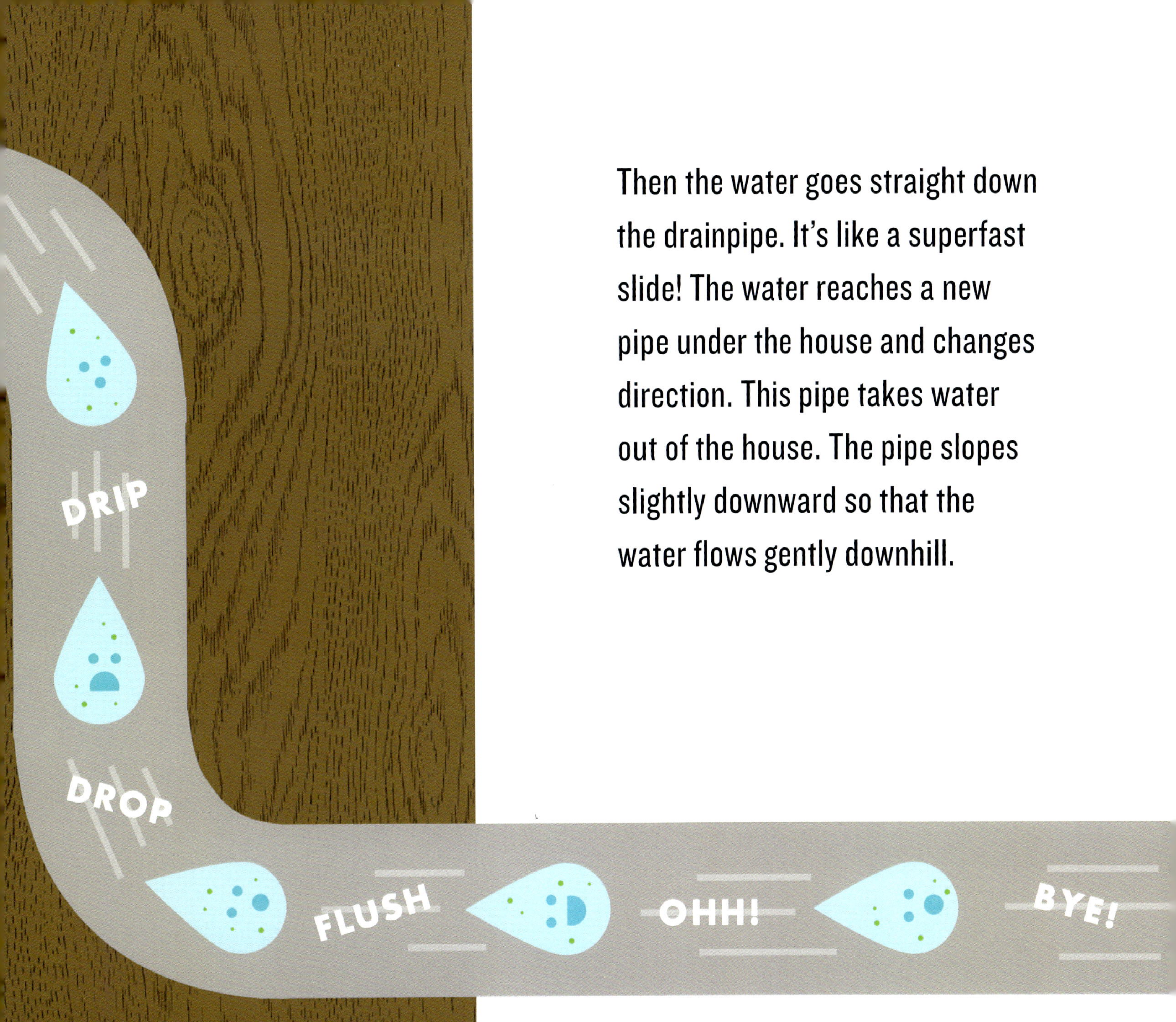

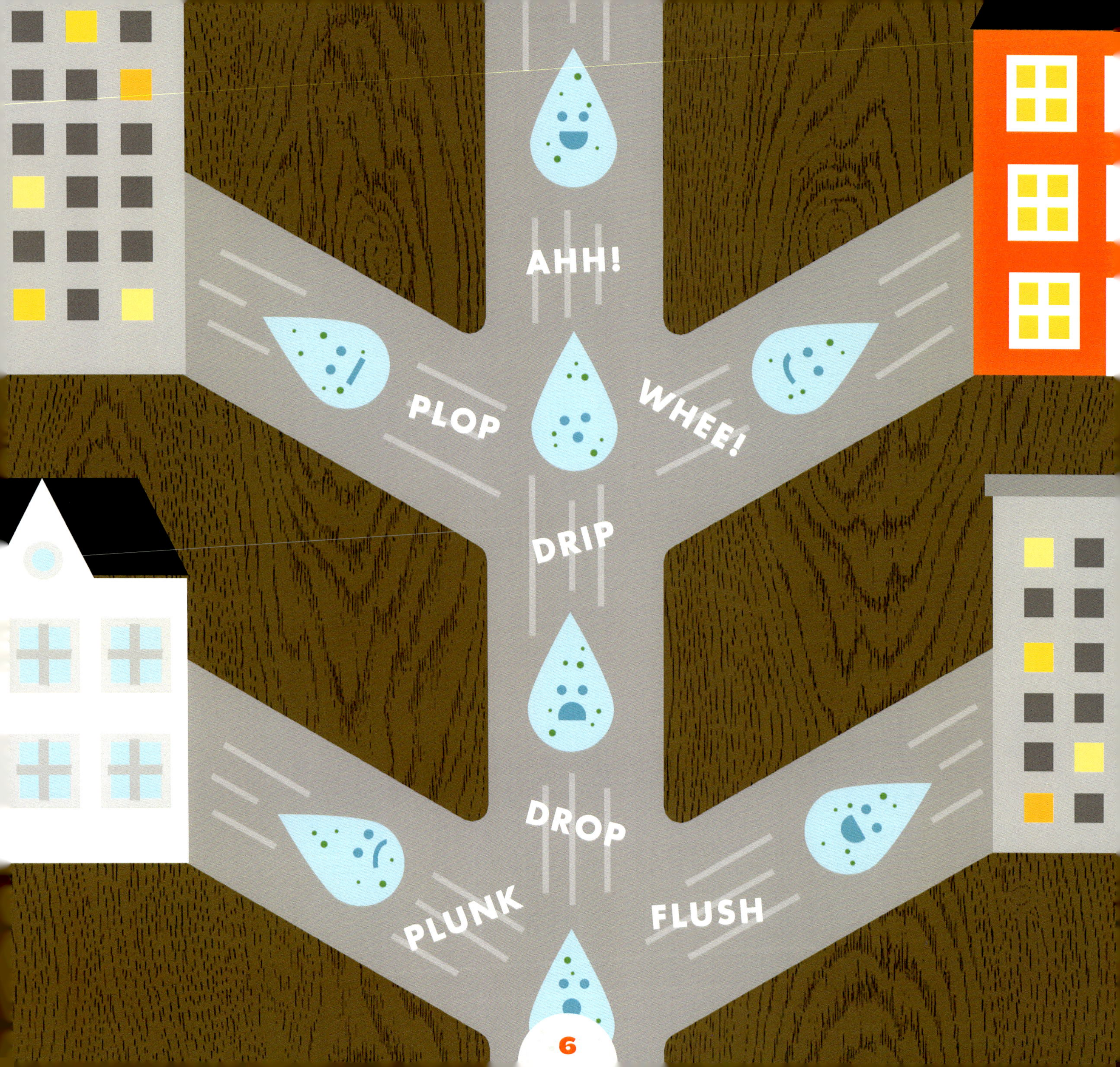
AHH!
PLOP
WHEE!
DRIP
DROP
PLUNK
FLUSH

Next stop: the city sewer. Here, your dirty dishwater meets dirty water from the other houses on your street. Sink water, bathtub water, washing machine water, and toilet water are all here. It's like a big stinky party!

All that dirty water eventually flows into a bigger pipe, where it meets even more dirty water.

Uh-oh! Party's over. The dirty water has arrived at the water treatment plant. Here, it will get clean. Hey, even bath water needs a bath at the end of the day!

First, screens catch big items like that lettuce leaf and the sock that escaped the washing machine. All this stuff goes to the garbage dump.

At the same time, grit settles to the bottom of the tanks. These are small but heavy pieces, like sand, eggshells, and coffee grounds.

Next, fat is skimmed off the top of the water by a big machine. The fat comes from foods like butter and cheese, which were in your macaroni and cheese.

NOW I'M
FAT FREE!

Now, tiny living things are put in the water. These microorganisms eat any food left in the water—like little bits of noodles that got washed down the drain. They also eat the dirty toilet water!

I GOT TOILET WATER!

Meanwhile, yucky stuff from the water is recycled. When the microorganisms eat, they leave behind sludge. This sludge is used as fertilizer to help plants grow.

Finally, the workers add special chemicals to disinfect the water, to kill any bacteria and other germs left.

All clean! The water flows through a pipe into the river. Ah, there's nothing like the great outdoors.

What if it rains? Rainwater doesn't need to be cleaned. It flows straight into storm drains that flow into rivers. That's why it's important not to throw trash into storm drains.

Later, the river water is collected, cleaned, and then sent through pipes to your house. It comes out of your faucet. So the same water may be used to wash dishes twice!

RECYCLE IT YOURSELF

MAKE YOUR OWN WATER FILTER

What You Need:

- Dirt
- Water
- Plastic 2-liter bottle
- Small rocks or pebbles
- Sand
- Cotton balls

For water to be used again, it has to be filtered and cleaned. You can make a simple water filter at home to see how this works.

What You Do:

1. Add dirt to the water (or use dirty dishwater).
2. Ask a grownup to cut the bottle in half.
3. Place the top half of the bottle in the bottom half, lid side down, so that it makes a funnel.
4. In the lid, build your filter. Layer the cotton balls, then the sand, and then the rocks.
5. Pour some of the dirty water over the filter. It will trickle into the bottom half of the bottle.
6. Compare the dirty water to the filtered water. It's not clean enough to drink, but you can use it to water flowers.

GLOSSARY

disinfect To clean by using chemicals to destroy bacteria.

fertilizer Material added to soil to make plants grow better.

microorganisms Living things, such as bacteria, that can only be seen with a microscope.

sewer An underground pipe that carries wastewater.

sludge Mud or muck, in this case coming from sewage.

storm drain A slot on the side of the street into which rainwater flows; storm drains usually flow into rivers.

water treatment plant An operation that cleans sewer water.

READ MORE

Allyn, Daisy. **Where Does the Bathwater Go?** New York: Gareth Stevens, 2012.

Staggs, Kelley. **The Story of Drinking Water.** Boulder, Colo.: American Water Works Association, 2011.

Walton, Ruth. **Let's Drink Some Water.** Mankato, Minn.: Sea-to-Sea Publications, 2013.

Yanez, Anthony. **A Wild Ride on the Water Cycle: An Alice and Jacob Adventure.** Houston, Texas: Bright Sky Press, 2014.

WEBSITES

Clean Water, Clear Choice: Kids

http://www.cleanwaterways.org/kids/

Play games and learn about school programs that teach how to how to keep our water clean on this site for kids by the Stormwater Management Joint Task Force in Texas.

Clean Water Education Partnership

http://www.nccwep.org/involvement/kids/index.php

Fun activities promote keeping storm sewers clean.

EPA: Learn About Water

http://water.epa.gov/learn/kids/drinkingwater/
gamesandactivies.cfm

Videos, games, and activities teach you all about water.

Wastewater: Sewage in Your Face

http://www.sandiego.gov/mwwd/general/kids/

Everything you ever wanted to know about sewage and more! Trivia, facts, and pictures will gross out your friends and help you learn about this important part of city utilities.

Every effort has been made to ensure that these websites are appropriate for children. However, because of the nature of the Internet, it is impossible to guarantee that these sites will remain active indefinitely or that their contents will not be altered.